HOW TO WRITE EROTICA AND MAKE MONEY DOING IT

The Complete Guide to Writing, Formatting, Publishing, Selling and Making Money with Erotica Short Stories on Amazon

Autumn Greer

Be sure to follow Autumn Greer on Amazon for notifications of new titles!

If at any time you find that you'd prefer to just write, rather than format your stories, I offer Formatting, Editing and Publishing services for my fellow Erotica and Non-Erotica Authors. Check out my website here for pricing and specifics, or contact me at RomanceAuthorCentral@gmail.com.

Enjoy and be sure to rate and review my books!

Contact me at RomanceAuthorCentral@gmail.com or visit my site at AutumnGreer.com

The information provided in this book is for the purpose of education. It is meant to give as complete an example as possible. No Part of this book may be reproduced in any form or by any electronic or mechanical means, including information storage and retrieval systems, without written permission from the author, except for the use of brief quotations in a book review.   Copyright ©
Romanceauthorcentral@gmail.com

Contents

Forward

Be warned all ye who enter here. This book is about sex. We are writing, describing, detailing and publishing erotica. With that being said, there will be some content in this book that is a little racy, lewd, sexual, erotic, carnal, obscene, sensual, suggestive, kinky, lascivious, erogenous and any other way you can say it.

Read, enjoy and follow the information in this book to get started writing Erotica **_Today_** on Amazon Kindle and Kindle Unlimited.

In this book you will learn:

Important Things to do Before You Start Writing
Programs to Help You Format and Publish Your eBook
How to Write Your Story
How to Format your Story for uploading to Amazon
How to Upload and Publish your eBook on Amazon

If at any time you find that you'd prefer to just write, rather than format your stories, I offer Formatting, Editing and Publishing services for my fellow Erotica and Non-Erotica Authors. Check out my website here for pricing and specifics, or contact me at RomanceAuthorCentral@gmail.com.

So, let's get started.

Why Erotica

When I was dreaming of being a writer in my younger days, I would have never imagined that I would become an erotica author. It's just not something that people dream about, or at least I hadn't.

Erotica is the only genre that I know of that a new author can get a short story written and sell a copy the first day its available. Its quick, its dirty, people buy it!

Sex sells. That is an age-old adage for a reason. People want sex. We need it. We crave it. We are biologically wired that way.

Now, I'm in no way saying we're all the same. We all have our kinks, what we like and dislike. This can be a small or big deal for each person. Some people might enjoy a wide array of erotica genres, others will only want one type of story, just told in a different way, or with new players each time.

The good news is that there are millions and millions of hungry readers out there, just waiting to click that buy button on whatever you'd like to write.

Why Short Stories

Erotica is the simplest genre there is to write. If you've ever had sex, you can write erotica. Writing good erotica, that keeps buyers following your name on kindle, and buying each new story is not as easy as just writing the first thing that comes to your mind.   You want to create a scene that keeps people wanting to know more.

You should write and publish regularly. I try to get stories out weekly when I am adding to my collection. No matter how fast of a typist you are, it can be draining hammering out a set word count each day, but you should to set a goal for yourself.

Short stories are the bread and butter of the Erotica Genre. Ten short stories, with a ten-thousand-word count, will be quicker to produce, quicker to write, and quicker to published and may be better selling than one 100k word count novel.

And you need product for sale for readers to buy!

The more books, stories and collections you have available the easier it is to hit your goal for page reads, sales or income each month.

Erotica doesn't need a long story line. You don't need ten chapters delving into your main characters childhood, or their education; your reader is looking for one thing if they have found your Erotica story.

They want sex.

The amount of fleshing out each character needs may vary, but if you have the basics (Age, Sex, Location, Vocation and Kink) you are usually good to go. Describe your character, but if you spend thousands of words detailing her breakfast, you've probably lost your reader.

How long should your story be?

Stick to a work count of around 10k per story (before you add your back matter or copyright word count to the total). This will give you enough material that the reader will know your character, and enjoy the smut.

 And don't make your story too short. If you do, your reader may feel ripped off by a 2500-word afternoon delight quickie. A 2500-word count is the minimum allowed to publish a story on Amazon. You might be the first to make a fortune on 2500-word count stories, but it's not common.

Collections:

With a 10k word count per short story, you will have a 30k word count collection if you only bundle three of your stories. We'll delve further into collections a little later on (as well as back matter and such) so don't worry, just focus on your goal.

10k words per short story is your goal.

Before You Write

There are a few things to get the hang of before you spend hours, or days pounding away at the keyboard. If you already have a story written don't panic, you can go back and work on these things before continuing with your finished short story, but trust me, it will make your life soooo much less painful if this all is taken care of ahead of time.

Before you start writing you need to: Create a Pen Name (or choose one of your existing ones); develop a formatted word document to use as a template for future stories; and Create a KDP (Kindle Direct Publishing) Account. I will tell you how to do each of these steps below.

Pen Name

Amazon allows authors to publish under one main account, with as many pen names as they would like. So you can have an account that you publish all your works, all your genres, all your kinks and so on under one email address, one pay check, one dashboard and one bookshelf (we will discuss these later on). I will explain dash board and bookshelf later.

So why not write it all under one name?

You need a pen name. We all do. If you are writing Erotica it is a necessity. Besides it giving you a layer of protection from people finding you or your loved ones online, it will also help you and your readers in another way.

How? You might ask…

The benefit of writing under various pen names helps you keep track of a certain genre or kink. Write all your paranormal erotica under one name. Write all your lesbian erotica under another. Write all your historical erotica under a third. Go crazy! Try out all the genres your heart (or other places) desires.

You can even group similar kinks under the same pen name. All Alpha type stories (male or female, dominant/submissive stories) under one. That's fine too! Just try not to get wildly different types under the same pen name.

This avoids the readers downloading a bunch of your stories, and getting something they didn't want. We never want our readers to get something they were not hoping to read. We want them loving every story we right in the genre/kink of their choosing.

Try to stick with easy to spell, easy to remember names.

Developing a Formatted Word Document

I write all my stories in a Word document. They are all generated from a paperback template that is available free through kindle.

You have two options here:

First Option, follow this link. Download the blank template and add aspects to it that you want in every one of your stories, like a Title Page, Copyright text and Backmatter (backmatter is where you link additional titles you write, link your review page and link your website, if you have one.).

Second option is to follow the step by step process on how to create your own template. Amazon has it all detailed here. This link is full of information on margin sizes, line indentations, and step by step instructions on how to create your own template. If you choose this route, be warned it will take some time.

Use either of the links above to download or create a template. Save it on your desktop. Write in it, save it as a new document under the new story's title.

My template includes:
     -A Title Page (Title, Subtitle, Author's name)
     -A Dedication Page
     -Copyright Text
     -A blank page for my Table of Contents (I add the Table of Contents in with Kindle Create, a free program that Amazon offers Here to fine tune your document's formatting for uploading to Amazon, we will discuss this program later on in this book. I recommend using it to finish your formatting, and optimize the document for Amazon. It is not necessary to use Kindle Create, I personally find it helpful. I will tell you how to add a

Table of Contents generated by Kindle Create in the Chapter discussing how to format your book with Kindle Create)
-Backmatter

I start every story from that template. That way all of my hyperlinks, all of my back matter, and my formatting is already done and waiting. I write in the document itself, and boom! Book is ready to go to Kindle Create.

Creating a KDP Account

You will need a KDP (Kindle Direct Publishing) Account to publish works on Amazon. Take some time to set one up. You will need to enter in tax info and a bank account for Amazon to send your royalties to (Ka-Ching!). Their process is pretty self-explanatory, so follow their steps and get one ready.

A Note on Word

I use Word because that is what I'm comfortable with. It's easy and simple for me because I already know how to do everything on it. I can add hyperlinks quickly. I can format chapter titles, and change fonts without thinking about it. I am used to it.

That being said, there are other options available to you. Scrivener is one. Some people swear by it. It's more complicated than I need, so I stick with my trusty old Word Doc. But explore, try other things out, and see which word processor works best for you.

No matter which word processor you decide to use, figure out how to create a template and do it. Trust me. You can thank me later!

Writing the Story

Okay! Your template is ready. You are ready to dedicate yourself to pumping out that 10k word count for your first short story! Now what?

Decide on a Genre or "Kink"

Kink. You'll hear that term a lot in Erotica. Kink is simply which subgenre of Erotica you are writing under. You've got to pick one before you start writing a story. You're not married to it, but try to keep similar kinks under the same Pen Name. Doing this will avoid readers/followers getting a surprise they didn't bargain for if they end up purchasing another of your titles and it is a totally different genre than what they were looking for.

For example, if you only ever write gangbang erotica about women getting drilled by a group of men, don't suddenly publish supernatural werewolf/shifter erotica under the same pen name.

Amazon will allow you as many pen names as you'd like (at least at the time of this writing) so use the tools you've been given and help to sort through the tons of stories you are going to write. See above about choosing a pen name.

A Simple Outline

While there are some people (myself included) who NEED an outline to get all their ducks in a row with more complex fiction, you don't need a huge one for an erotica story. Sex is simple. Erotica is simple. Keep it simple!

The basic outline I try to follow is:

-A Teaser of Scenes to Come
-Before the Act
-Meeting the Other Participant(s)
-Setting the Mood
-The Act
-Conclusion

And that's all you really need. Now, we'll go through and detail each step.

If this sounds too much like a formula to you, by all means do your own thing. Write it your way. This is *your* story, *your* pen name, and there are no rules.

Teaser

Any good book needs a hook. This is erotica, you already have the hook set up for you. Write the best part of the kink you're writing about. The hottest moment that makes your heart go hell yeah. Put it here.

We want the reader to not be able to put your story down; whether they downloaded your title from kindle unlimited or are reading the sneak peek, a preview of your book that Amazon automatically generates (and this preview is usually the first few pages of your book). We need them to *HAVE* to turn the page and keep reading.

With most of my titles I do this by detailing the start of the 'Act' or when they are just about to get down and dirty, but that doesn't always have to be the case. You can catch a readers attention simply by giving them questions in the first few pages of your story. Questions that they *need* answered.

You have to have a killer hook for the readers to keep reading, don't skimp here. We will go over a few examples below.

Teaser Examples

Below, we will go over three examples of teasers. We will then discuss what makes these excerpts keep the reader turning the page, and finishing your story.

Teaser Example 1:

Shelly looked out the car window, towards the small building with the neon sign; underneath which, was the half silhouette of a nude woman.

"We can really go in there?" she asked nervously.

"Yes. If that's what you want. You can have exactly what you told me." His voice was clear. There was no doubt expressed.

She hesitated for only a moment, "OK. Let's go."

Questions from Teaser 1

So, what is the hook in the above excerpt? Are there questions asked? Why does your reader keep reading?

Hopefully, if I've done my job you want to know who the woman and the man are; what the woman wants; and why they might be able to find that thing she wants at a club, sporting a neon sign of a nude woman.

Teaser Example 2

Janice sat on the foredeck of the forty-foot houseboat. It was dusk. The automatic lights on the dock had just come on. She held a very strong gin and tonic in her hand. Her friend Vickie was roaming the boat, nervously drinking her own brew, something with too much rum. Vickie made her way to the foredeck.

"Do you think he will really show up?"

"He'll be here." Janice replied.

"How do you know? I can't believe you actually called him."

"I know him."

"Just how well do you know him? What haven't you told me?" Vickie pleaded, half laughing.

"Well enough."

A black Porsche pulled into the parking lot.

"He's here."

Questions from Teaser 2

Who is the man? What are they waiting for? Why is he coming to their boat? What hasn't Janice told Vickie?

Anna knew she should stop, but when the caller ID showed his name, she remembered the last time. And the time before that. The money was good, she told herself.

It was only a couple of times a month. That didn't make her a whore. They had even dated. Once.

At the end of the evening, she was enamored and completely at ease with him. He had walked her to her door, held out his hand as if he was going to shake hers, taken her hand, raised it to his lips, kissed it, and still holding her hand, had raised his eyes to hers. His proposal had caught her off guard. He'd said she was beautiful. His eyes had seemed to light with a high altitude, atmosphere blue brilliance. In a color she had never before seen.

"I'd like to see you again. But under different circumstances."

Her doorbell rang.

Questions from Teaser 3

What is Anna doing that she shouldn't? Who is the man? Is he paying her to do something? Under what different circumstances does he want to see her again?

Before the Act

This one's simple. Set up the scene before they meet the person (or persons) they're about to get hot and heavy with. Depending on the story, this can be detailing an average day, or what led up to the event, but this is where we make the situation believable.

Show your character, give a little detail about them and their situation, and make us relate to them. Age, Sex, Location, Vocation, Kink.

And, though this should be obvious, try to set the scene in a place where your characters would be. If you are writing a Western Erotica, don't put your Cowboy/Cowgirl in the middle of a jungle (unless that is part of your story). Depending on your Genre/Kink, if the situation is too fantastical your reader might be put off.

For example, a Werewolf might be commonplace in a paranormal erotica. But you shouldn't randomly put one into a story about a MILF banging her pool boy.

Meeting

Again, this one is pretty self-explanatory. Introduce the main character to who they are about to bang. Depending on the genre you are writing this can go a bunch of different ways, but our goal is that the reader not only thinks they might get it on, the reader should *demand* they do the deed.

If you're writing a Romantic Erotica story, they could have a cute meeting, or immediately have a deep connection with one another.

If you're writing a Boss/Secretary story, the Boss might have just hired the secretary, or she/he might have been hired by a temp agency.

If you're writing a dom/sub story where the sub's kink is to be fucked by random strangers, you probably don't have to devote much time into the sub meeting their partner(s); however, subs generally have an attachment to at least one person in the scene (most likely their dom).

My advice on figuring out what your kink/genre commonly uses to introduce the characters is to read that kink/genre. Find titles that are performing well in that category and read as many as you can. Not only will it give you inspiration, but it will also show you something about your competition.

Setting the Mood

This is where we build the desire. We want the sexual tension so thick, that they are choking on it (in a good way). Make the main character want and need the release as much as your readers now do.

This is Erotica, so while we want it believable use a little creativity here to set the scene so that your reader is in the same frame of mind as your character.

Let's be honest, our readers are buying erotica for a very specific reason. They want to be turned on and they want to get off. The buildup is more important than anything (as any woman will tell you) so don't wimp out here.

Are they in a bedroom? Are they in an office? A car? A park? A hallway in a club?

Use all of your senses to describe the foreplay, and the scene. Feel the bedsheets beneath your character. How does her partner smell? How do his hands feel? Are they rough or gentle? Is the action rushed or slow?

Use oral, and use it well. Imagine the last time you gave it to someone, and describe every action. What made them go wild? What made them moan? What did the sounds *they* made do to you? If you can't remember specifics, it might have been a little too long since you last partook. If you have a willing partner, do some research (wink-wink).

The Act

Guess what? This is where they get it on. Do the deed. Bump uglies. Fool around. All that and what have you.

There are only so many ways to write these scenes, but if you did your job in the build up to it, this part should be easy. Again, use all your senses to describe the scene.

What is your character feeling? Hearing? Touching? Tasting?

There are endless ways to describe the multitudes of acts and aspects of what people do in their bedrooms. Use every sense available and make them count.

Conclusion

This can be as short or as long as you'd like it to. I have had some stories that have pages to wrap them up, I have had others that took a few sentences. The story will tell you what it needs. If it feels half-assed to you it probably is. Write what you need to, to conclude the story. Leave it open ended if you'd like, but finish the story.

Do they go to breakfast?

Does he call her a cab?

Does she kick him out and slam the door?

Whatever you decide on make sure it fits and finishes the story.

How to Beat Writer's Block

Erotica authors have an endless supply of free research available, only a few moments away. The best way to come up with new material is to watch porn. I know, our jobs are terrible!

Spend a little time exploring your genre in live action. Get some inspiration from the thinly veiled plots of a few videos.

If that doesn't work, and you are stuck in a story, try changing the setting. You wouldn't believe how much it helps a story get rolling. Rather than always being in a bed, stick a couple of characters in a business, a parked car, or hell even a Coffee Shop. The setting is as much a character as the players in your story. Use it to your advantage.

The Most Profitable Kinks

There are a lot of kinks, and a lot of readers, but some genres stand out among the rest.

The most purchased genres that I have written and sold in are:

Alpha Male Erotica

Multiple Partner Erotica (Gangbang; Threesome and such)

Lesbian Erotica

Romantic Erotica

Exhibitionist Erotica (Public sex)

These are the easiest to sell, but also the most competitive to get into. Make no mistake, there are tons of other people out there writing and selling erotica. You need to get quality and quantity above them. You can do it in any kink, but it's easier to do it in one that you actually enjoy.

Other Types of Kink

Here is where I will list a lot of genres for you to choose from. These Kinks/Genres are subgenres of Erotica that are on Amazon and are selling NOW. Choose any that strike your fancy and try it out!

Action & Adventure; African American; Alpha Male; Angels; BBW; BDSM; Bikers; Billionaires; Cowboys; Dark; Devils/Demons; Fantasy; Ghosts; Historical; Horror; Humorous; Interracial; LGBT; Mystery; Paranormal; People in Uniform; Poetry; Rockstars; Romantic; Science Fiction; Shapeshifter; Suspense; Thrillers; Urban; Vampires; Victorian; Werewolves; Westerns

There are more, but those are the most prolific available on Amazon.

Editing

Editing is tough. Because this is Erotica, and you are writing under a pen name, you will probably start out editing your own stories. That's fine. Just be aware you will miss stuff, and autocorrect will miss mistakes. Take a day away from a story after you finish it, before you edit. This will let you have some distance from it, and reduce the amount that you skim through the story. Take your time with your edit. Believe it or not, even readers of erotica desire a well written, grammatically correct (as much as possible) story. Read it slowly. Flesh it out. Pay attention. Because your reader is paying attention. If your writing appears sloppy, and that you don't really care, neither will your reader. And your next title may go unread.

Important: Edit AFTER you have the whole story finished.

If you are having an issue with continually missing mistakes and are at a loss as to how to catch yourself, try contacting another self-published erotica author. Perhaps you can trade editing help. Or ask your partner, if you're brave enough to share your stories with them. A fresh set of eyes will do wonders to help catching those pesky little typos.

I would, however, recommend you not ask friends or family to edit your erotica stories. Stick to your fellow authors, your partner, or pay someone. If you pay someone to edit your works for you, you can remain anonymous.

I offer editing services for my fellow Erotica and Non-Erotica Authors. Check out my site here, for pricing and other services, or email me at RomanceAuthorCentral@gmail.com.

Backmatter

Backmatter is the stuff the end of each book. You've seen it a hundred times, and unless you loved the story you've probably skimmed over it. This is where the author puts links to other titles, asks for a review and rating, and in general tries to make their next sale to you (the reader).

Backmatter is one of the only ways for you to promote your erotica. USE IT! Put back matter in every story, every collection, and make sure you link each title. Go to the sale page on Amazon for the title you are linking, copy the URL from the address bar, select the title name in your back matter, click add hyperlink, and paste the URL you copied for the specific title.

Do this in your template as you add titles to your catalogue. Don't skip this. This is VERY important.

Make the next sell (teaser or excerpt)

A little trick I found after I had already written and published a number of titles was this, add an excerpt or teaser for one of your other titles at the end of you book. The reader is in a reading type of mood (hopefully, if you've done your job well) so use it to your advantage and hook them on another one of your titles, before they put the first one down. LINK THE TEASER BOOK BEFORE AND AFTER THE EXCERPT!

Formatting the Book

You have your first story written. The word document is already formatted. You've edited once, at least. You're ready to publish right? Not quite.

In this chapter, we will discuss the things you need to do before you publish on Amazon.

If at any time you find that you'd prefer to just write, rather than format your stories, I offer Formatting, Editing and Publishing services for my fellow Erotica and Non-Erotica Authors. Check out my website here for pricing and specifics, or contact me at RomanceAuthorCentral@gmail.com.

Edit in Your Word Processor

This will save you a lot of stress later on, do ALL of your editing in your word processor. Add all your hyperlinks. All your back matter and summaries ready. Add in your page breaks. Make Chapter titles bold and in a larger font size than the rest of the book body. Make sure everything is ready to go before you go any further. We will finish formatting in Kindle Create below.

Kindle Create is great for optimizing a finished product, but it is terrible at editing that document.

If after following the steps below, and your book is published, and you then notice a mistake you need to correct, make sure you do those edits in your word processor, and re-format the document in Kindle Create after the Word document is up to date and edited to your liking. When it is 100% and ready for readers, then continue to Kindle Create.

No one told me this when I was starting out, and trust me I did my research! Kindle Create does not allow you to go backward in file format (for example: Create a PDF or other type of file from the Kindle Create File). So if you ever want to promote your book in a different format, you will have lost all the editing you have done in Kindle Create.

<u>Do all of your editing in your Word Processor.</u>

Format in Kindle Create

Kindle Create is a free program offered by Amazon, available for PC and Mac. Here is the download link. You need 4+GB of Ram on your computer/laptop; Windows 7 or Later for PC; MacOS 10.9 or later for Mac. Kindle Create is available in: Dutch; English; French; German; Italian; Portuguese; and Spanish. Follow the Link above, download either the Mac or PC program depending on what you're using and install.

This program is great for formatting the document to upload onto Amazon, but do all of your Edits before you start in Kindle Create.

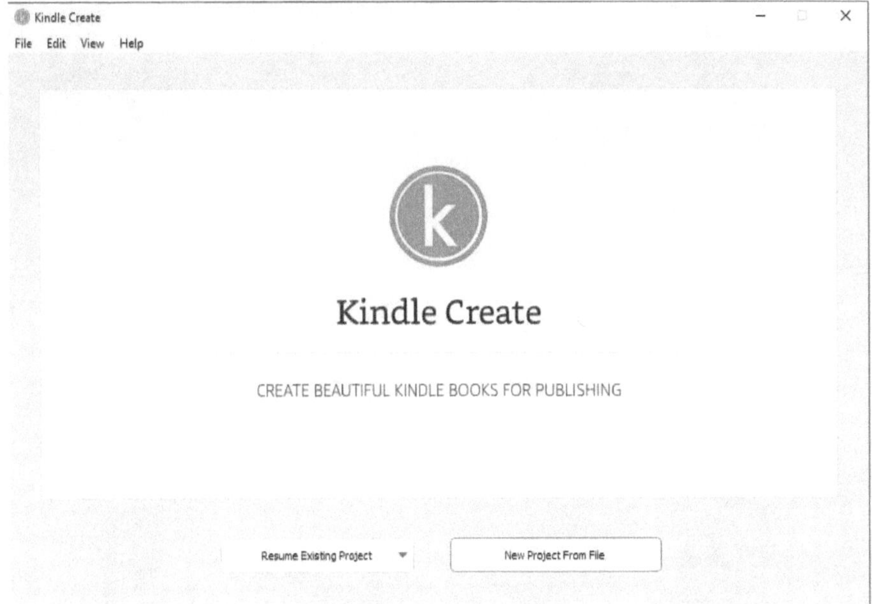

To import a document into Kindle Create start Kindle Create from the short cut on your desktop or in your programs menu. On PC the shortcut symbol is a light blue circle with a white "K" in the center. When the program window boots up you will have two options: "Resume a Project" you already are working on (by clicking the left dropdown menu button) OR use the right button to create a "New Project from File".

Since this is your first one, you will click the "New Project from File" button. From the next window choose the upper button (labeled Novels; Essays; Poetry; Narrative; Non-fiction) as your short story should be text heavy, not picture heavy.

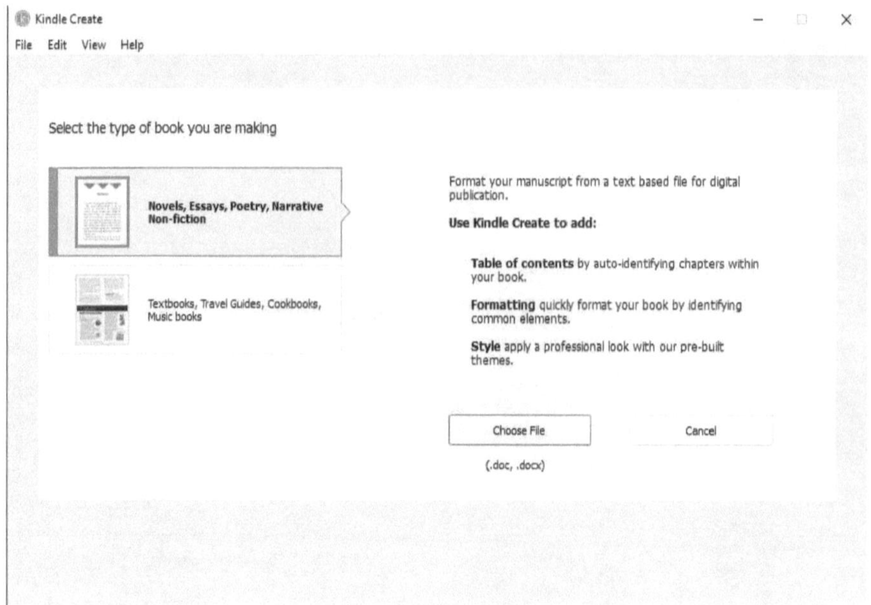

This is what you will use for almost everything you format through Kindle Create. Next, choose the "Choose File" button and find your document that you are importing into Kindle Create.

Now you need to:

Assign Element Formatting to Aspects of the Book

When your document is uploaded into Kindle Create it will ask you to continue, then give you a chance to select Chapter Titles from a list of choices it guessed at from your documents original formatting.

If you made sure to bold and increase the font size of your chapter titles in your word processor before importing the document, it should have guessed those for you. Most often, it will also randomly choose your title, author name and possible a line or two from your back matter as possible Chapter Titles, simply uncheck the boxes next to those choices, then click the "Accept Selected" button, and it will automatically format those chosen selections as Chapter Titles. Formatting Chapter Titles is helpful for generating a Table of Contents later on.

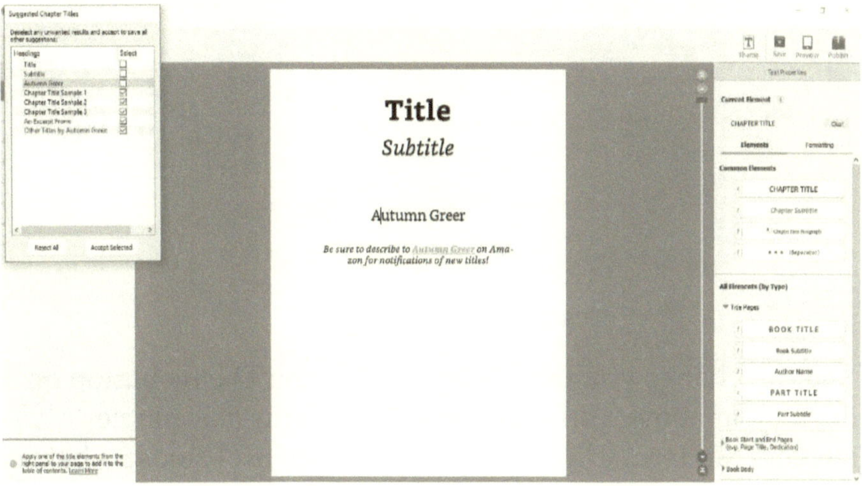

Now that you've gotten that far, you will see your document as it is currently formatted. Now we need to refine that formatting. Don't worry, after you do this a few times, you will be able to do it in your sleep.

On the left, will be a window that will list each aspect of your book as you add formatting to it (for example: chapter titles; dedication; title page; table of contents, etc.). At the center of the window will be your story as it is formatted now. To the right, you will see options to add formatting to your story.

Kindle Create will automatically apply a theme to your document. A "Theme" is a set of specific fonts, and text sizes for elements of your formatted eBook. "Elements" are aspects that are already formatted through the theme you choose to apply to your title, should you choose to apply a different one from what Kindle Create automatically applied.

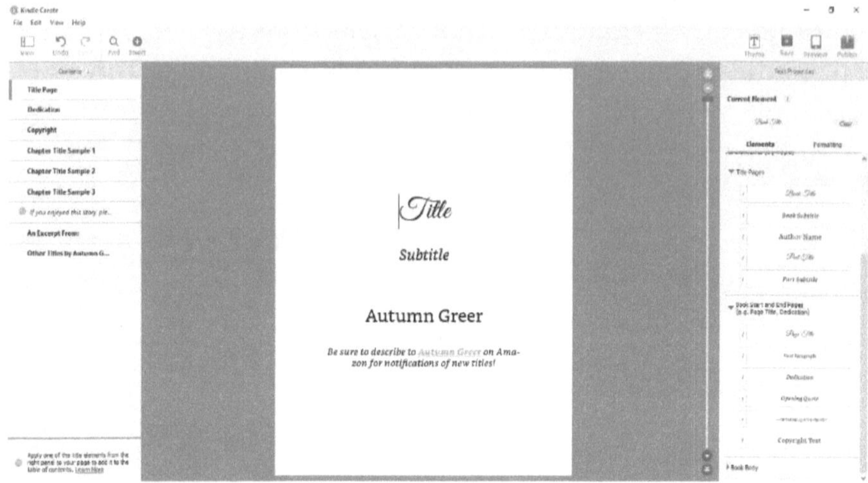

You can change your theme by clicking the Theme button on the toolbar above your story preview. Themes available include: Modern; Classic; Cosmo and Amour. Choose what fits your story.

To save your title as a Kindle Create project, click the save button to the right of the Theme button. Name the file and save it. If you'd like to view a preview of your work, click the Preview button next to the Save button. The "Publish" button, furthest to the right, will be the last thing you do in Kindle Create so wait on clicking that.

We will now continue with the formatting of your title. Select your Main Title Text and click the "Book Title" element in the right option menu, under the "Title Pages" drop down menu of the Kindle Create window. Select your subtitle (if you have one) and select the "Book Subtitle" element below the "Book Title" Element in the formatting section of the window.

Continue to add each Element formatting option to each aspect of your book that it applies to.

Under the "Title Pages" element drop down menu, you will have the options of: Book Title; Book Subtitle; Author Name; Part Title; & Part Subtitle.

Under the "Book Start and End Pages" drop down element menu, options include: Page Title; First Paragraph; Dedication; Opening Quote; …Opening Quote Credit; & Copyright Text.

Under the element drop down menu titled "Book Body", options include: Chapter Title; Chapter Subtitle; Chapter First Paragraph; Block Quote; Poem; & "***(Separator)".

You might use a lot of these, you might not. In most of my eBooks I use: Book Title; Book Subtitle; Author Name; Dedication; Copyright Text; Chapter Title; & sometimes Page Title.

When formatting collections, I might also use: Part Title for each subtitle of each story added to the collection. I'm going to tell you later on how to Format several of your stories together into a collection.

Experiment with the Elements, see what you like, but try to format all of your titles in the same way so that they look the same for your readers.

If you accidentally add an element format to somewhere you didn't mean to (for example: added the element format of Book Title to your pen name, instead of the actual title) simple select the text, and click the CLEAR button in the upper right portion of the Text Properties window (the window on the right side of the Kindle Create window). It will remove the text element and you can add a different one, or leave it formatted the same as the body text (the default setting).

Add Table of Contents

After you get all of your elements formatted, go back up to any spot between your title page and the first chapter of your book, and click the "Insert" button (+) on the left side of the upper tool bar. This will give you the option of inserting a table of contents or inserting a picture. Click Table of Contents and Kindle Create will automatically generate one according to the Elements you applied to the file.

Be sure you do this AFTER you have already assigned all of the element formatting to your document (for example: title, subtitle, copyright text, dedication, chapter titles, part titles and such). If you forgot to mark a chapter title or an element you want shown in your Table of Contents, delete the Table of Contents that you already inserted (delete it just like you would delete a word you didn't want in a sentence), add the element to the desired content, then generate a new table of contents following the steps above.

Publish

Click save. And now you are ready to click the Publish button. Don't worry, this won't stick your book up on Amazon for you. This will simply create a finalized file, optimized for Amazon, for you to upload to Amazon Kindle Direct Publishing when you're ready to publish your title for sale.

Cover Page

The hard part is done. You have your story written, and formatted to upload onto Amazon KDP. Now we need a cover.

Amazon offers a cover generator through KDP. You're welcome to do this, but these usually look a little elementary. And we need sales! We want a cover that sells our book the moment a hungry shopper dives into the search bar, looking for your kink.

Where do you get one?

Well, you can buy one through Fiverr, an online website where you purchase a service (such as creating a Cover Page) but again these are not the gorgeous fiction covers you see on your favorite author's books. They're usually lackluster. You can purchase better covers through online services (myself included) or there's another option.

So, where then?

Make one yourself!

Photoshop

Adobe Photoshop is a godsend. If you can afford it, buy it. It makes cover creation so much simpler. You can pay for a yearlong license for $120, or pay per month for a subscription (either option is way cheaper than it used to be when I was still in school). We will discuss how to use it to create a stunning cover below.

If you can't swing the payment for Photoshop, download Gimp. It has a lot of less features, and is harder to get the hang of, but it will do in a pinch.

Amazon has formatting guidelines for cover pages just like it does for the book itself, so check them out and make your cover according to those.

This is another great time to create a template to make your life easier later one. Do it.

Check out other Erotica Covers for inspiration. Try not to follow the crowd too much though, as you want to stand out. Create a sexy cover that catches your reader's eye and makes them click on your link.

Stock Photo Sites

There are tons of Free stock photo sites for you to download images of attractive women and men. They might not be exactly what your looking for, but its better than nothing and they're FREE!

Search, and download. If you don't find what you're looking for, then pay for a subscription to a higher-end stock photo site, and download as many as is allowable by the subscription you purchased. Think of ones that would get you to buy a book in the genre. Download those and format them into a cover. Check out other authors covers and decide what you like looking at.

Creating the Cover Page

Since I use Photoshop, I will be showing you how to create a cover in Photoshop. Many of these steps are applicable in other programs, but since I don't use any other programs than photoshop for cover creation I can't make any promises.

Create <u>Another</u> Template

I'm sure you're getting tired of hearing this, but a template is your friend. A little work ahead of time creating one will help you in the long run. I am going to go through the steps for creating a cover page template in photoshop and show you how I made the cover for this book!

Purchase Photoshop if you haven't. Follow the link, sign up for the license (length of use, either monthly or yearly) and pay for it. Download the program. Install the program.

If you already have it, great!

Open up photoshop, and create a new document. Follow the size and resolution guidelines in the image below. A Width of 6 inches (or 1800 pixels); a Height of 9 inches (or 2700 pixels) and a resolution of 300 pixels per inch.

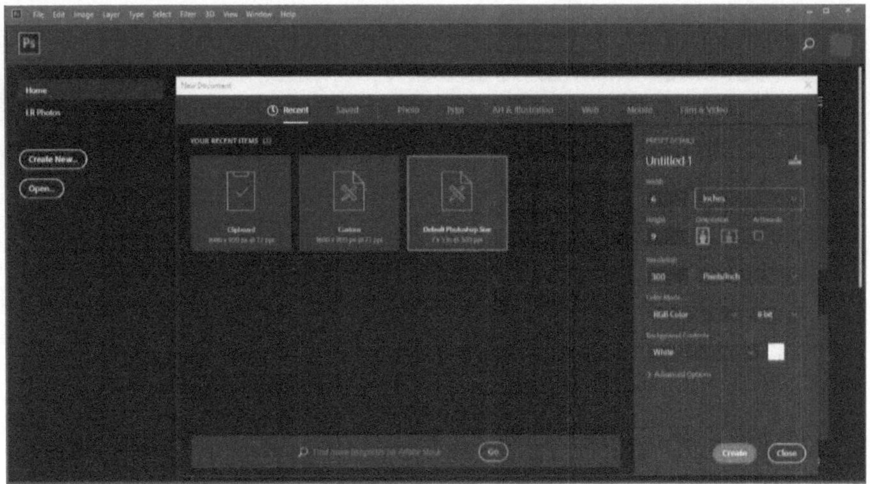

Photoshop will generate a new blank white page document of the correct size guidelines if you follow the options above.

Save this as your template.

Finishing the Template

To create the cover, and add other elements to it (such as our title, subtitle, and the cover image/art), we will use photoshop to create layers in the file.

First, we will add the Main Text to your title page. Click the text tool icon on the left toolbar (the text icon is a "T"). If you don't see it, photoshop has a quick trick to selecting a specific tool. Look at the upper right corner of your window. Find Magnifying Glass icon there, this search bar will allow you to search for a specific tool. Click the magnifying glass icon, type in "Text tool" and photoshop will automatically select the tool. I believe the proper name for the text tool is "Horizontal Type Tool", but text tool will work just fine.

When the Text tool is selected, click where you want your Title on the cover (don't worry you can move this around later) and type the title there. Because we are still making a Cover Template File, I will use "Title". Repeat these steps to create a Subtitle and Pen Name text line on the Cover page. Your Template File should look like this:

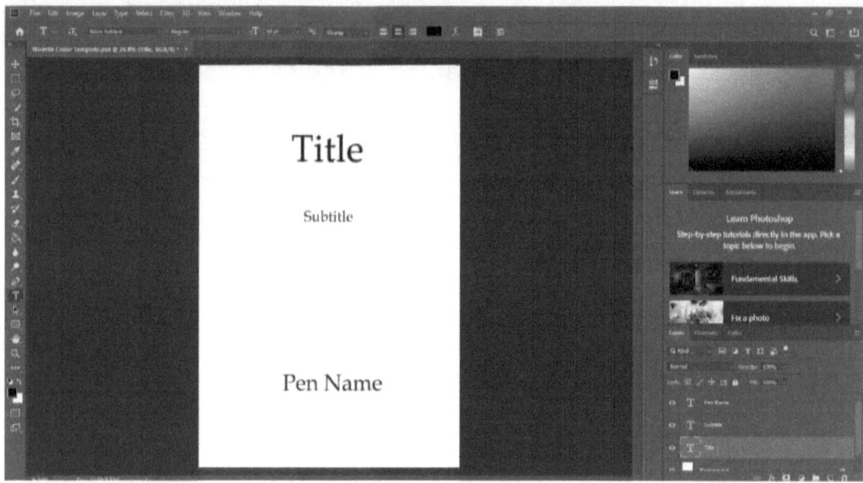

Save that as "Cover Template" or whatever title you'd like. That's your template. To create a new file from the template, click File, then "Save As" and title the file as the "Cover Page for (insert the title of your story here)". For this tutorial, I'll name it Cover Page for Example.

Next, we will use this starting point to create the cover page for your title.

Creating Your First Cover

With your new file open, we will start with adding the Title, Subtitle and Pen Name into the template. Use the text tool, select Title, and replace it with the title of the story you're making this Cover page for. Then repeat the steps for Subtitle, and Pen Name.

Remember that you have to include your Title and Subtitle as it will appear on your eBook on Amazon in the Cover Page, so follow it word for word. Here's mine so far.

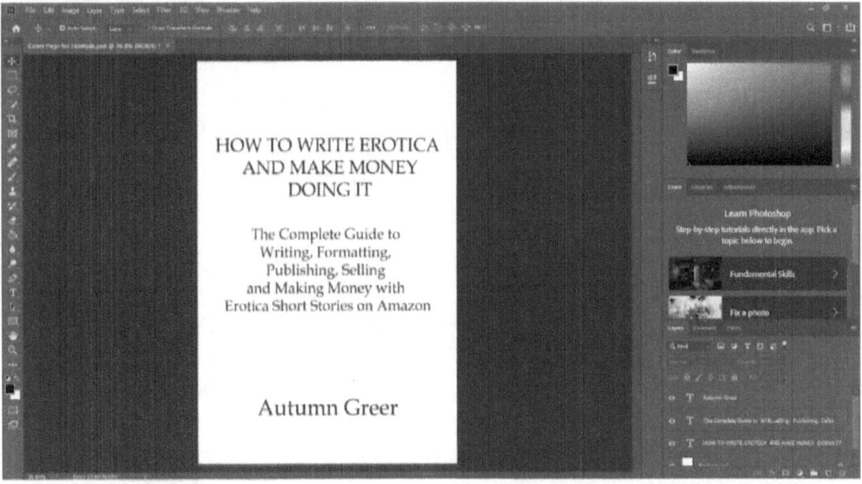

I know, I know, that's a long title and subtitle, but it's the name of my books, so its got to be there. Notice the window at the bottom right of my window, it says "Layers" and lists a title for each layer. This is important for the next step.

Next, we will add the main image of the Book Cover Page to the Photoshop template. If you don't have some sexy stock photos yet, get to searching. When you have the one you'd like to use for the title you're working one, get back to photoshop and open the file. Select the File drop down menu in the upper left corner of the window, click Open and select the desired image. When the file is open, simply drag the Layer from the photo's window, to the title tab of the cover window.

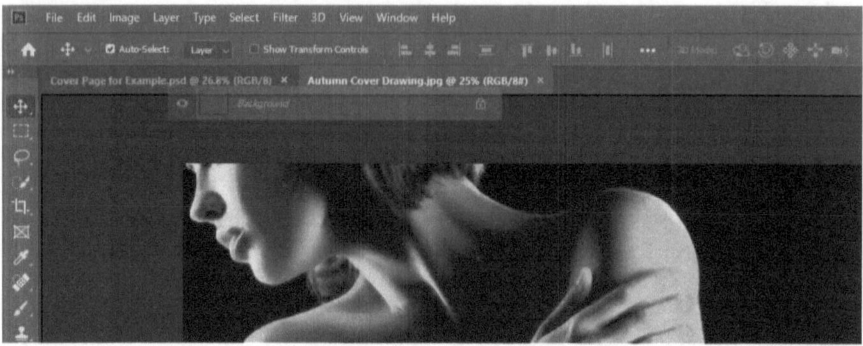

When the image is dropped onto the cover file, it will probably cover up the text. Select the Image Layer from the Layers window and click and hold, then drag that layer below the other ones, for the text you've already added to the cover. Like so:

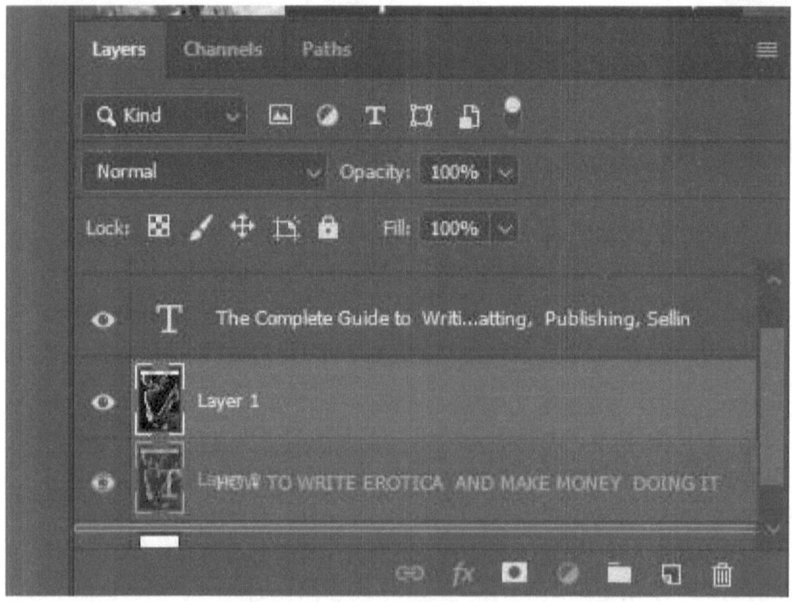

You may need to resize the image and drag it around to the desired look. After it is how you want it, you may also have to change the text color. Simply select the text tool, select the text, and change the color tile on the text tool bar at the top of your window. This will take some time, but keep moving, changing and editing until your cover fits the vision you had for it.

After a few changes in font, a filter and adding a rectangle background for my title and subtitle, here is where I'm at with my cover.

To add a rectangle behind text: click on the rectangle took (at the bottom of the toolbar on the left side of your window) if you can't find it, don't panic, just simply use the magnifying glass to search for it in the upper right corner of your window. Click the magnifying glass icon, type in "rectangle tool" and photoshop will automatically select the tool.

As you can see, I used colors from the main cover art to make the background of the text flow with the cover art. To select a color from an image, click the eyedropper tool, or the color swatch from your left side tool bar. Then simply click the color you want from the image. You can choose to alter the color (make it darker or light) then click the ok button and that color will be used for all shapes (like the rectangle) that you make from there on out. If you want to change the color of a previously made rectangle, select the Fill tool (or search for it with your search tool) and click on the rectangle you want to change the color of. If you do this and the fill tool changes the color of a different part of the image, rather than the rectangle, you have the wrong layer select. Select the layer for the rectangle and use the fill tool again.

When you are happy with your Cover, you will need to export the Photoshop file to get it into JPG or TIFF formatting (these two file types are the only ones Amazon Kindle Direct Publishing will allow). To do this, click the File menu drop down, find Export As… in the drop down. Click that. Choose to export it as the desired file (I usually do a JPG) and save it in a location you will be able to find it at.

There you go! A finished Cover!

Creating a Collection

Collections, or Bundles, are the gold mines of Erotica. You will LOVE collections! Readers LOVE collections! Collections give your readers more bang for their buck. They are more likely to hit that buy button when they are getting a bundle of stories instead of just one. It also works at keeping Kindle Unlimited readers entertained, and turning the page for the next story, as it's all in one tidy file on their eReader. Which means more pay per page reads for you!

Below we will discuss how to create a bundle of your stories, and how to format these treasures.

To Create a Collection, you will need at least three finished short stories of a similar Kink. I have seen bundles that are totally different kinks, and if your readers enjoy your writing enough, they might not mind a little variation, but I find collections of similar titles sell the best. You can have more than three stories in a bundle or collection, as many as you'd like, but at least three.

Formatting a Collection in Your Word Processor

To format a collection, I use the same template I use to make any Erotica story. Open the File, and Save As… title the new document under the name of the Collection. Your main title should be the name of your collection. You can use titles from different Pen Names, or short stories all from the same Pen Name. If you use stories from multiple Pen Names, list them all on the Cover Page.

You will need to make a Part Title Page for each short story. I copy and paste the finished short story into the word document, and head it with a "Part Title Page" for that short story. For the Part Title Page, I usually just list the Title and Author name, then start with the story.

Follow the same formatting guidelines for a short story (Bold and increase the size of each chapter title).

Repeat the above steps for each short story. Create a Part Title Page with the short story's title and Author Name; Copy and paste the finished, edited story after the Part Title Page. Format the Chapter Titles.

When you have done this for each short story you are including in the collection, go through and edit the title again, just to be sure that there are no grammar or spelling errors you missed before. If you catch any new ones, be sure to update the short story's original word processor file as well.

When this is all done, you're ready to format the collection in Kindle Create. Save and close your word processor document.

Formatting a Collection in Kindle Create

Formatting a collection in Kindle Create is very similar to formatting a short story in Kindle Create. Import the document as a new project and select your chapter titles from the automatically generated list Kindle Create offers you. Be sure to deselect the Main Title of the Collection, all instances of the Author's name, and each of the Short Stories Titles.

When this is done, click the Accept Selected button.

Now, go through and format the document much as you would a short story. Choose the Theme you want. Format the Collection's Title as your "Book Title" Element. Add the element formatting options to your subtitle, pen name(s), copyright text, and dedication.

The additional step for collections is to format each of the Short Stories Titles as a "Part Title". Do this and you are ready to insert your Table of Contents, somewhere at the start of your book (I most often do this just after the Copyright Page).

After you're all done with your formatting, save the file as a Kindle Create Document, then click the Publish button to finalize the file.

When this is done, you will follow the below steps to get your collection on Amazon, just as you would for any other Short Story.

Getting Your Title on Amazon

You've created your Finalized Kindle Create word/content file (Amazon will call this your Manuscript). You have a striking Cover Page. Now we need to get your erotica story uploaded to Amazon. Here we go.

You will need a KDP (Kindle Direct Publishing) Account. Take some time to set one up. You will need to enter in tax info and a bank account for Amazon to send your royalties to (Ka-Ching!). Their process is pretty self-explanatory, so follow their steps and get one ready. When you do. Continue on.

Now You're Ready to Get Your eBook on Amazon

When you have followed Amazon's steps and have your KDP account finished, you are now ready to take the steps to get your eBook published. If you're not all ready logged in, log into your KDP account. Click on the "Bookshelf" tab option. This will take you to your Bookshelf. This is where KDP will list all the eBook you're going to get published on Amazon.

Click the "+ Kindle eBook" option and we can start!

There are three pages of information you will need to go through to get your title ready for review, and published. I'm going to walk you through those three pages.

Kindle eBook Details Page

First, you will have to fill out the "Kindle eBook Details" Page. I'm going to explain each section and how to fill them out below. This is where you will: choose the Language of your title; Enter in the Book Title and Subtitle (these have to appear on the Book Cover); Series Information (if you are publishing a part of a series); Edition Number (if you are editing a title); Author Name (Or Pen Name); Description of your book (your blurb to sell your title); confirm your publishing rights; Enter Keywords; choose Categories; and you will ignore the Age/Grade Range option (I'll explain why below); and decide if you're ready release your book as soon as possible or want it to be available for pre-order.

Most of the aspects of this page are pretty easy to figure out. Enter your title in the title section, your subtitle below that in the subtitle section. Choose the language your book is written in from the dropdown menu. Below we will discuss the not so obvious parts of this page.

Series Information is used to connect your book to others in a series, this will show up under the details section on the purchase page your readers click on. If you have a series following a character, you should fill this part out. If not, leave it blank.

The Edition Number is used to specify different editions of your title. If you are adding edits, or making major changes to your eBook, add a number in there so you can keep track of major edits. You can enter in 1 if you'd like since this would be the first edition of this specific title, or you can leave it blank.

Under the Author section, where it is labeled Primary Author or Contributor, enter in your pen name, first and last in their respective fields. The below section for Contributors is where you would add other author names if this book is a collaboration of more than one author, or if there was a co-author involved. If you are writing under a pen name do not add your real name in either section as it will be visible on the finished purchase page of your eBook.

The Description section of this page is where you will write your blurb. A blurb is a summary and teaser of your eBook. This needs to be given as much time as your story was. This is what will sell your book, after the prospective readers clicks on your fantastic cover. Make it work for you. I usually try to write a short, medium and long length blurb for each story, then choose my favorite (usually the longer of the three) to place here.

In the Publishing Rights section you will simply select one of two choices. If you are publishing an erotica title you dreamt up and wrote and you hold the publishing rights to the story, select the top bubble, indicating that you own the publishing rights. If you are publishing a work that is in public domain, you can also sell these on Amazon. That's a whole different book. If you'd like to read more about publishing a work that is under public domain, click here.

Next we have Keywords. This is extremely important, and may require some research. At the end of this book, I've added a section with Example Keywords (check those out). Select ones that fit your story. Be aware that the more popular combinations of Keywords will have more competition, so get creative, and think of what you might enter into a search in Amazon to find a story like the one you have written. Put those here and fill in all of the available space you have. The more the merrier.

Amazon allows you to choose two categories. I usually select Erotica (under the Fiction drop down menu) and Erotica (under the Fiction, then below the Romance drop down menu). We will discuss ways to get additional categories at the end of this book under Keyword Examples.

The Age and Grade Range section should be left alone if you are publishing Erotica. Oddly enough, Amazon does not consider Erotica Adult Only Content, and you don't want your works labeled as Adult only. If it is, it will never come up under a search, and will make it very difficult for you to make a profit with the title. Amazon won't notify you that your title has been labeled as Adult. The only way I have found to quickly check this is to visit SalesRankExpress.com, and search your pen name. Below each eBook, there will be a Content Rating. If your Content Rating is "Safe" you're good to go, if your Content Rating is "Adult" you will need to edit the Cover (make sure there is no nudity) and blurb of your eBook, then contact Amazon and ask to have it reviewed, to have the Adult Rating removed.

The last section on the first page of publishing your book is the Pre-order Section. If you want your book released as soon as possible, click the top bubble, stating "I am ready to release my book now"; if you want your title held as a Pre-Order, click the bottom button and specify the date you want the title released by.

eBook Content Page

The Second page is for your eBook Content, we will again explain each section below, these sections include: Digital Rights Management (we will explain this below, this can only be altered before the title is published); upload your manuscript; upload or create your cover page; view a preview of your eBook; & Enter an ISBN.

The "Manuscript" section is where you will first select if you would like to enable Digital Rights Management, or not, and then where you will upload the file you formatted through Kindle Create. Digital Rights Management makes it more difficult for the book to be pirated, but not impossible. It also makes it a little more difficult for your work to be shared (through household sharing, an option Amazon allows to customers), and can also make it impossible for a customer to read the title if they are using a non-kindle device. I normally do not apply the Digital Rights Management as I feel if a person hits that purchase button, they should be able to enjoy that work on any device they choose, even if its not a Kindle. Choose wisely as you CAN NOT alter this decision after the title is published. When you decide on that, choose the respective option, then upload your formatted Kindle Create file (the file we 'Published' through Kindle Create). When the file is uploaded KDP will run a general spell check, but its not as trustworthy as your own editing and Word processor, so don't rely on it too heavily.

Your Kindle eBook Cover will be the next file to upload. If you created a file through Photoshop, export it to a JPG or TIFF file (as this is all KDP will accept) and Upload it here.

When both the cover page and manuscript files are uploaded, you will be able to generate a preview of your title. If you'd like to view it, click Launch Preview button. It takes a while to generate.

The last section on this page is the ISBN section. eBooks are not required to have one. You can purchase one and add it here but KDP automatically generates a free ASIN number, so I just use that. An ASIN is an Amazon Standard Identification Number, which is used by Amazon and its partners to identify your eBook.

eBook Pricing Page

The third Page is all about your eBook Pricing. We will go through each section below. This page includes: KDP Select Enrollment (90 days enrollment minimum); Territories your book will be released in (all territories for example worldwide or individual territories) and your Royalties and pricing. You will also have the option of enrolling in Kindle Matchbook, I will explain that below, allowing kindle book lending and then you must agree to the terms and conditions.

The first section on your third and final page to publish your story, is the option to enroll in KDP Select. This allows people who have purchased a subscription to Kindle Unlimited to read your title for "free". You will be compensated per page read of your title. Do this if you would like an additional revenue stream. All of my titles are available through Kindle Unlimited, as I feel that Kindle Unlimited users and general purchasers are two separate groups. There are so many titles available on Kindle Unlimited that the readers could read untold amounts of Erotica, and still never need to purchase another story. To be eligible for Kindle Unlimited your title must be exclusive to Amazon in digital format. This means it is available only through Amazon, but can be read on other eReaders.

Next you will select the territories your book will be released in (all territories for example worldwide or individual territories that you select) and your Royalties and pricing. KDP gives you the option of choosing 35% or 70% royalties of each copy sold of your eBook, depending on the pricing you select for your title, and will automatically calculate the exchange rate of the price you set. Between 2.99 and 9.99 USD you will earn 70% of each sale. Below or above that margin and you will earn 35% of each sale. After you enter the price for this specific title, KDP will input the calculated exchange rate for that price depending on the territory. You have the option of clicking on the "Other Marketplaces" drop down menu below "Primary Marketplace" and altering the automatically generated price of the title in each territory so that is a more eye appealing number, or one that the purchaser is more used to seeing in their marketplace. For example, if KDP calculates the price of a title from 2.99USD to 3.59 CAD, you could change the CAD total to 3.99 CAD.

The next section is for you to choose if you will enroll your title in Kindle Matchbook. This is optional, and only useable if you are planning to also create a paperback version of this title. To do that, your story must have at least 24 print pages. I normally don't bother with creating a paperback version of my erotica stories as they just don't sell compared to the eBook Versions. But if you do choose to create a paperback version, Matchbook allows a purchaser of your paperback version to download the eBook version for an additional cost (between $0.99-$2.99).

Book Lending is next. If you are in the 70% royalties bracket this is not optional and the checkbox will be locked.

The last section on this page is accepting the terms and conditions. And a disclaimer stating it can take up to 72 hours for your title to appear on Amazon from the moment you click the "Publish Your Kindle eBook" button.

When all pages are completed, you can click the publish button! And now you just have to wait for the title to go through approval. This can take up to 72 hours but normally it is pushed through between 4-12 hrs.

KDP Dashboard

Your Kindle Direct Publishing Dashboard is where you can view, edit and mange your titles, view reports, search community forums and view your KDP Select Enrollment. Here we will go over all of these options and discuss their uses.

Bookshelf

This is where all of your titles will show up. They are sortable and searchable. All titles you publish to your KDP account will be viewable here, no matter which Pen Name you publish them under. Each title will have the option to edit its content, Keywords and details, as well as create promotions and sales.

This is also the page where you will start each new title.

Reports

Your Reports page will detail all of your royalties, sales and monies you have earned. On this page you can also generate more detailed reports and instantly convert the selected data to different forms of graphs, for your viewing pleasure.

There is also the option of viewing the new KDP Reports Beta, which has more information, options and more details than the general reports tab. Check it out, its quite intuitive, and informative.

Community

The Community tab will take you to the KDP forums where you can search or post and take part in discussions with other authors. I spend too much time writing, and not enough time online to tell you much about the Community on KDP but they are always there to help and discuss!

KDP Select

The KDP Select tab will detail KDP Select (enrolling your book in Kindle Unlimited) features and options, and direct you back to your Bookshelf for you to enroll titles into the program if you haven't already done so while publishing your titles.

All the Other Stuff

After your book is published you have a few other things to do to set each title up as a productive member of your bookshelf.

Promotions

To find the promotion options for any given title, go to your Bookshelf and scroll down to a published title. When the title is published, a "Promote and Advertise" button will be on the right side of the title window.

Erotica titles are not currently permitted to run Ad Campaigns through Amazon. But we have other options! When enrolled in KDP Select (Kindle Unlimited) a title is eligible for Kindle Countdown Deals and Free Book Promotions.

Kindle Countdown Deals allow you to create sales for each title. You can set a window of time that the title goes on sale for from its original price, and even different increments of sale prices. For example, you can put a $2.99 short story on sale for $0.99 for three days and set the promotion to automatically increase the sale price to $1.99 for two days after the first three days are up. Countdown deals get your title into different categories, and the more people buying and downloading your title the better!

Free Book Promotions are exactly what they sound like, they allow readers to download a specific title for a specified set of days for Free. Why do you want to give a book away? Do this to hook readers onto your stories, get your Pen Name noticed, and get reviews for a new title!

Reviews

Reviews are hard to come by for erotica titles. A lot of people are worried if they leave a review someone might know they read the Erotica story. There are ways to leave reviews anonymously, but most readers won't review your stories organically.

I have had some success with free book promotions. Review sites are available, where you give away a PDF, Mobi or Epub copy of your title in exchange for the possibility of a reader review. Most of these sites get about a 1/5 return rate (meaning you have to give away at least five copies to get one review) but one review can earn you a lot of readers!

I have tried various sites, but my favorite is Booksprout. It offers a free option (giving away 20 copies), and automatically reminds readers to review.

You can not require a review for a free copy of a book. Amazon is very adamant about this. As they should be! We don't want phony reviews on products we buy, we want real information. So if you write a good book, and get a good review great! If not, you might hook a new reader who will have to buy the rest of your titles to get more of your stories. Win/Win.

Here's where I remind you to review another writer's stuff as well. If you download a story, book or collection, for research, entertainment or any other reason, and you enjoyed their work, drop them a rating at the vary least. As writers, we need to support our fellow authors, and hopefully we are able to knock out a paragraph or two about a book we enjoyed or learned something from. Open up your kindle and drop a few reviews and ratings for titles you haven't done so with yet.

The Big Secret

Well, it's not so much a secret, but you need to keep writing! Write as many short stories as you can, and get those titles onto Amazon. When you have a bunch of the same genre short stories use collections to get more of your titles in the hands, and eReaders of your adoring public.

Give yourself a daily goal, either word count, page count, or just producing something. Stick to it. If you don't set a goal, you will get bored, or put off working. Even with a day job, you can produce short stories with KDP.

Keep producing great content!

Keep publishing new stories!

And keep earning those royalties!

If at any time you find that you'd prefer to just write, rather than format your stories, I offer Formatting, Editing and Publishing services for my fellow Erotica and Non-Erotica Authors. Check out my website here for pricing and specifics, or contact me at RomanceAuthorCentral@gmail.com.

Keyword Examples

Below are keyword examples that I often use and have had success with. Remember to only use Keywords that apply to your story. You want readers to find your work, and get what they expected.

Also be aware that Amazon has some keywords they require to catalogue your Erotica into certain Subgenres. You can find out more about that here. I find that if you choose your keywords wisely for what your story is about, you usually end up using the keywords they require to get into a specific category anyway so don't worry about that too much.

Adult	Cowboy	For Women
Alpha	Coworkers	Forced
Anal	Cuckold	Gang
Angry	Daddies	Gangbang
BBW	Daddy	Ganged
BDSM	Dark	Gay
Billionaire	Discipline	Graphic
Bisexual	Dom	Group
Books	Dominant	Historic
Boss	Domination	Hot
Breakup	Ebook	Husband
Bundle	Erotcia	Interracial
Camping	Erotica	Kindle
Cheating	Ex	Unlimited
Club	Exhibitionist	Lesbian
Collection	Explicit	LGBT
College Student	Femdom	Love
Combos	FF	Menage
Cougar	First Time	MILF
Couples	For Men	Military

MMF
Naughty
Novels
Office
Older Man
Older Woman
Paranormal
Porn
Prime
Public
Punishment
Revenge
Rockstar
Romance
Romantic

Science Fiction
Second Chance
Sex
Shared
Sharing
Shifter
Shorts
Slave
Spanking
Stories
Stories
Story
Sub
Submissive
Swap

Swapping
Taken
Threesome
Transgender
Vampire
Virgin
Voyeurism
Werewolf
Western
Wife
Wife
Work
Young
Young Woman
Younger Man

Thesaurus

This section is full of synonyms for oft used terms in Erotica. Hopefully, this helps someone over an overly repetitive section of their book. There are obviously a lot that I am not listing, but these are ones that I have come across most often, and are commonplace in Erotica works. The most common synonyms will be in bold under each heading.

Woman

Lady, Girl, Chick, Filly, Dame, Broad, Bitch, Damsel, Wench Matron, Lass, Gal, Doll, Babe, Tart, girlfriend, she, her

Breasts

Bust, bosom, **chest**, mammaries, fun bags, **tits**, titties, teats, chest, boobs, tatas, bazongas, headlights, nipples, cans, gazongas, girls, hooters, twins

Vagina

Vag, clam, muff, mound, beaver, bush, **clit**, coochie, cooter, muffin, lady parts, lady bits, cum dumpster, **pussy**, **cunt**, taco, love lure, kitten, flower, **center**, lips, whispering eye, vuvla, trim, twat, snap, snatch, **womanhood**, box, fur pie, taco,

Man

Guy, dude, sir, husband, boyfriend, spouse, fellow, he, him, his, gentleman

Semen

Cum, sploodge, cream, juices, love seed, seed, baby batter, milk, nectar, nut butter, sauce, spooge, sperm, spunk, swimmers, wad

Penis

Cock, **dick**, pecker, baby maker, sword, beef, sausage, chubby, hard-on, dong, erection, staff, pipe, main vein, johnson, love muscle, meat, **manhood**, rod, pole, wood, one-eyed monster, phallus, package, schlong, shaft, snake, wang, wiener, willy

To Come

Cum, climax, bust, come, cream, explode, blow a wad, bust a nut, get off, orgasm, pop, shoot off, spurt, unload

Sex

Intercourse, go to bed, hump, fuck, bone, screw, sleep with, go to bed, take someone to bed, bump uglies, do it, couple, do the dead, breed, copulate, procreate, do the nasty, fool around, get laid, get some, go to bed, hook up, make love, lovemaking, mate, nail, play, whoopee, the horizontal tango (or other dance), poke, knock boots, pound, root, rut, shag

If you enjoyed this How To, please leave a Review or Rating
to let me **know**!

Follow Autumn Greer on Amazon for notifications of new
stories, and visit us at AutumnGreer.com
If at any time you find that you'd prefer to just write, rather
than format your stories, I offer Formatting, Editing and
Publishing services for my fellow Erotica and Non-Erotica
Authors. Check out my website here for pricing and specifics,
or contact me at RomanceAuthorCentral@gmail.com.

Other Titles by Autumn Greer:

Be sure to follow Autumn Greer on her Author Page Here

Titles featuring The Man:

The Club: A Game of Choice

The Man visits The Club, a swingers' club. There, he is asked to join a Game of Choice by a Porn Star. Three Husbands get to spend time with the Star. Three wives get to choose three mystery single men from The Club to spend 60 seconds with, then choose one to spend thirty minutes with. Will he be chosen?

The Club: A Married Woman's Debut

A husband goes to The Club without his Wife, so she does the same. While there she meets The Man. Will this be her first and last time at The Club? Or will she be its newest regular?

The Club: Submissive

The Man brings a friend to The Club, and she's all tied up. With three couples, three single men and The Man, what's a girl to do?

The Visitor: An Anniversary Gift

Annie's husband finds her search history by accident, and arranges to have her deepest fantasy become a reality. Joel finds a Visitor who can grant these desires, in ways even Annie didn't think was possible. The visitor shows this couple what true passion can be, and takes the lead to make this Anniversary Gift one to remember.

Titles featuring other Alpha Males:

A college student hears of a place that the woman is in control of the night, and allowed to make her wildest fantasies come true. She's never done anything like this before, but will a night with three men be the liberating experience she's been waiting for?

An irresistible neighbor, named Vlad, asks Sarah to water his plants while he is away. Inside, she finds a locked door. What's behind that door is more enticing than she could have ever imagined. Behind Locked Doors will show you what Vlad is hiding and leave you begging for more!

Business Affairs Book 1 & 2

Corinne thought she had seen the last of Paul, but on the night celebrating her biggest success he shows up, bring back memories of their first night together. An encounter she will never forget. Will this be the last she sees of him?

Paul offers Corinne a new experience. This one with two stunning blonde women. Will indulging in what she thought was a forbidden desire give Corinne the confidence she's been lacking?

Victoria's two best friends drag her out to a performance by a band she's never heard of, and boy is she glad they did. When the drummer of the band only has eyes for her will Victoria take a chance that is totally out of character for her, and see where it leads?

A jealous neighbor tries to move in on Tina's boyfriend, with Tina there, but her boyfriend has another idea all together for the night.

Changing Jobs & Changing Partners
Cherry has no choice but to fire Dylan. But as he's leaving, she realizes this might be her last chance to find out if he wants her as much as she wants him.

They're both married, and now she is his ex-boss. This can't turn out well. Or can it? Dylan invites Cherry and her husband to dinner at his house, with his wife. His very attractive, very bisexual wife. What happens when you swap partners with your ex-employee? What happens when that employees wife wants you and your husband?

Speed Dating
A handsome stranger takes a lucky speed dater out for the experience she never knew she needed. A business man named Tony, a mysterious club within a club, and a live performance that involves dropping all the barriers she has ever had. Stephanie learns that excitement can come from the least likely places, and along the way she might learn a little about herself and what she's been missing.

Stop and Go
She has had enough of her soon to be mother in law calling her a whore. If she thought she was a slut, then she would be one! A truck stop on the way how is sure to be the most exciting stop her and her fiancé have ever had!

Romantic Erotica

The Coffee Shop

After breaking up with her cheating boyfriend, on the drive home from a business trip, Nessa meets and falls for a handsome Army Ranger. Will this chance meeting be their one and only time together? Or is this the start of something to last?

The Job Interview

Ellie needs this job. She's behind on every bill she has, and she is so damned close to finishing her degree she can taste it, but when her interviewer is not only the most handsome man she has ever laid eyes on, but also the most interesting, is she having dinner with him to secure her position in the company? Or looking for something else entirely?

Time Goes Slowly

Charlotte is bored. She tired of the same old too-polite, quiet guys, the same old dates, with terribly droll conversation. And she is determined to make a change.
When she finds an ad online, describing not only what the mysterious poster wants to do to her, but what he expects her to do while he does it, she is intrigued. Will he be the change she so earnestly craves?

Titles Featuring Alpha Females:

Sleeping with the Enemy

Sasha has something Bart wants, and Bart has something Sasha wants. Bart agrees on one condition: Sasha must spend two nights with his Dominant wife, Annette. Sasha has always wanted Annette, but will she be able to give herself over fully to the other woman's will?

Collections:

The Fantasy Collection: **Forbidden Desires Brought to Life Steamy Erotica Short Stories** (Amateur Night; The Club: Submissive; & Behind Locked Doors)

Suddenly Taken Collection: **Erotica Stories to Spend The Night With** (Changing Jobs & Changing Partners; Speed Dating; Stop and Go)

The Stranger: **A Collection of Intense Erotica** (The Visitor; The Club: A Game of Choice; The Club: Debut; A Neighbor Comes Calling)

Sweetly His: **A Collection of Romantic Erotica Short Stories** (The Coffee Shop; The Job Interview; Time Goes Slowly; and a sneak peek at Business Affairs 1)